Mama Lisa's Christmas Around the World

Mama Lisa's Christmas Around The World

Original Material Written by Lisa Yannucci

Translations by Monique Palomares and Lisa Yannucci

Additional Translations by Our Many Correspondents

Compiled and Edited by Jason Pomerantz

Visit Mama Lisa on the web at www.MamaLisa.com

© 2012 by Lisa Yannucci

Contents

Introduction

PART 1

1 The Holiday Season

2 Saint Nicholas Day
(December 6)

3 Saint Lucia's Day
(December 13)

4 Saint Thomas's Day
(December 21)

5 Epiphany
(January 6)

6 Saint Knut's Day
(January 13)

PART 2

7 Christmas Songs and Traditions From Around The World

8 Tu scendi dalle stelle

You Come Down From The Stars

(Italian Song)

9 Tomtarnas Julnatt

The Gnomes' Christmas Night

(Swedish Song)

10 Traditions: Colombia

11 Good King Wenceslas

(English Carol)

12 Patapan

Willie Take Your Little Drum

(French Song)

13 Huachí toritó

Giddy-up, Little Bull

(Bolivian Song)

14 Traditions: Holly

15 Fum, Fum, Fum

Twenty-Fifth of December

(Spanish and Catalan Song)

16 Traditions: Occitan

17 Nadal Tindaire

Jingling Christmas

(Occitan Song)

18 Wassail Carol

Also called Gloucestershire Carol

(English Song)

19 Leise rieselt der Schnee

Softly Falls Each Snow Flake

(German Song)

20 The Twelve Days of Christmas

(English Song)

21 Traditions: Provence

Les Treize Desserts de Noël

(The Thirteen Desserts of Christmas)

22 O Tannenbaum

O Christmas Tree

(German, French, and English Song)

23 Jest 'fore Christmas

(English Poem)

Introduction

Christmas is the most beloved holiday of the year for many children – and their parents!

In America we all know that Santa Claus delivers presents to good little boys and girls. We all know the cannon of beloved holiday songs like Silent Night and Jingle Bells.

But other countries and cultures have their own traditions and songs! And sometimes the celebrations take place on days other than just December 25!

This book is divided into two parts.

In the first, we discuss some of the traditions that take place on days other than Christmas itself. We find it fascinating to learn the stories of St. Nicholas Day, St. Knut's Day and all the others.

In the second, we present favorite Christmas Songs and traditions from a wide selection of countries and cultures.

Many of the sections in this book have links to our web site where you can often find recordings, videos and scores.

We hope you enjoy reading this book as much as we enjoyed putting it together. It's impossible to study this material without being infused with the joy and good will of the season.

We know there are many traditions and cultures that we were unable to include here. If you have a suggestion about something to add or any comment at all please write us. We'd love to hear from you!

You can contact us and find many, many more songs and customs at our website www.mamalisa.com.

Merry Christmas!

1 - Part 1
The Holiday Season

2 - St Nicholas Day
December 6

About St. Nicholas Day

December 6 is St. Nicholas Day. St. Nicholas was a bishop who lived in Myra, Turkey, from around 280 A.D. to December 6th, 342 or 343. His greatest legend is that he gave gifts to poor children.

There's one specific legend surrounding St. Nick about an impoverished man who had three daughters. He was so poor that he couldn't feed them and he decided that he had no alternative but to sell them into slavery.

The legend has it that St. Nicholas heard about these children. He sneaked over to their house at night and quietly left three bags of gold. One for each girl. He tried to sneak away, but the father saw him and praised his generosity to everyone.

In the 1100's AD, in France, some nuns started giving gifts to children on St. Nicholas Day. That's when the custom of gift-giving in December was established. Now some people celebrate the gift giving custom on St. Nicholas Day and others on Christmas Day.

St. Nicholas Day in Holland

Kirsten Kerkhof wrote me the following about St. Nicolas Day in Holland...

"In the Netherlands, Christmas is not as important for children as Sint Nicolaas (Saint Nicholas) on December 5th. It's on this day that children get their presents, instead of on Christmas Day. Sint Nicolaas is the patron saint of children. He is said to come from Spain, although the real Sint Nicolaas came from what is now Turkey."

In November St. Nicholas arrives on a steamboat from Spain, with his helpers and his white horse. Children go to watch his arrival.

Zie Ginds Komt de Stoomboot (Look, There is the Steamboat)

Here's a song they sing in Dutch, with an English translation...

Zie Ginds Komt de Stoomboot

(Dutch Song)

Zie ginds komt de stoomboot,

Uit Spanje weer aan.

Hij brengt on Sint Nicolaas,

Ik zie hem al staan.

Hoe huppelt zijn paardje,

Het dek op en neer,

Hoe waaien de wimpels,

Al heen en al weer.

Zijn knecht staat de lachen,

Hij roept ons reeds toe.

Wie zoet is krijgt lekkers,

Wie stout is, de roe.

Oh, lieve Sint Nicolaas,

Kom ook toch bij mij,

En rijd toch niet stilletjes,

Ons huisje voorbij.

Look, There is the Steamboat

(English Translation)

Look there is the steamboat

From far-away Spain.

It brings us Saint Nicholas,

I can see him, waving.

His horse is a-prancing

On deck up and down,

The banners are waving,

In village and town.

His servant is laughing

And tells everyone,

The good kids get candy,

The bad ones get none.

Oh, dearest Saint Nicholas,

If Pete and you would,

Just visit our house,

For we all have been good.

Many thanks to Kirsten Kerkhof for contributing this song and for her helpful comments.

Web Resources

You can find more kids songs from Holland (The Netherlands) here:

www.mamalisa.com/world/holland.html

St. Nicholas Day in Poland

Ed Gawlinski wrote to us about his family's holiday traditions. His letter shows how you can be creative and expose your children to many different customs around the world at this time of year...

"Lisa,

The Polish Custom is for Saint Nicholas (świętego Mikołaja) to bring children presents on December 6th .... The traditions that go with this parallel those in Germany, Austria, and elsewhere in Europe. I found a short poem for Saint Nicholas that you might enjoy."

Na świętego Mikołaja (On St. Nicholas Day...)

Na świętego Mikołaja

(Polish Poem)

Na świętego Mikołaja,

czeka dzieci cała zgraja,

Da posłusznym ciasteczko,

Złe przekropi różeczką.

On St. Nicholas Day

(English Translation)

On St. Nicholas Day,

The band of children waits;

For the good cookie he brings,

But for the naughty a switch that stings.

Thanks for sending us this poem Ed!

Web Resources

You can find more kids songs from Poland here:

http://www.mamalsia.com/world/poland.html

St. Nicholas Day in Belgium

Rudy Welvaert wrote to us...

"Every year, in the night of the 5th to the 6th of December, Saint Nicolas brings presents to all the children who have been good. That evening children put out a shoe in front of the fireplace and put a carrot or a turnip in it for the horse of Saint Nicolas. Saint Nicolas also has a servant, he's pictured as a black man (not very politically correct in our days, but that's the tradition). His name in Dutch is "Zwarte Piet" (Black Peter). The tradition of Saint-Nicolas is in both the Dutch speaking part of Belgium, Vlaanderen (Flanders) and Holland very similar. And many songs are sung by the children."

Here are some of the St. Nicholas Day's Songs Rudy sent us:

Sinterklaas Kapoentje (Saint-Nicolas Little Rascal)

Sinterklaas Kapoentje

(Dutch Song)

Sinterklaas Kapoentje,

Leg wat in mijn schoentje,

Leg wat in mijn laarsje,

Dank je Sinterklaasje!

Saint-Nicolas Little Rascal

(English Translation)

Saint-Nicolas Little Rascal,

Put something in my little shoe,

Put something in my little boot,

Thank you little Saint-Nicolas!

Here's a longer version of Sinterklaas Kapoentje (Saint-Nicolas Little Rascal)

Sinterklaas Kapoentje - Long version

(Dutch Song)

Sinterklaas Kapoentje,

leg wat in mijn schoentje.

Een appeltje of een citroentje.

Een nootje om te kraken,

dat zal wel beter smaken.

Dankje Sinterklaasje!

Dankje Sinterklaasje!

Saint-Nicolas Little Rascal - Long Version

(English Translation)

Saint-Nicolas Little Rascal,

Put something in my little shoe,

A little apple or a little lemon,

A little nut to crack,

That will taste much better

Thank you little Saint-Nicolas!

Thank you little Saint-Nicolas!

(Note: This is the song that Santa sings with the little Dutch girl in the beloved holiday movie Miracle on 34th Street.)

Saint Nicolas, Patron des écoliers (Saint Nicolas, Patron Saint of School Kids)

Rudy wrote…

"…in the French speaking part of Belgium, La Wallonie (Wallonia), the children are waiting for Saint Nicolas to bring them sweets and presents in the night of the 5th to the 6th of December. Here is a traditional Saint-Nicolas song in French, with its English translation."

Saint Nicolas, Patron des écoliers

(French Song)

Saint Nicolas, patron des écoliers,

Apporte-moi du sucre dans mon petit panier.

Je serai toujours sage comme un petit mouton,

Je dirai mes prières pour avoir des bonbons.

Venez, venez Saint Nicolas!

Venez, venez Saint Nicolas!

Venez!

Venez!

Venez Saint Nicolas!

Tralala!

Saint Nicolas, Patron Saint of School Kids

(English Translation)

Saint Nicolas, patron saint of school kids,

Bring me some sugar for my basket.

I'll will always be good like a little lamb,

I always say my prayers, to get sweets.

Come, come Saint Nicolas!

Come, come Saint Nicolas!

Come!

Come!

Come Saint Nicolas!

Tralala!

Hoor de Wind Waait (Hear How the Wind Blows)

Here's a another St. Nicholas Day Song from Belgium – This one from the Dutch speaking part:

Hoor de Wind Waait

(Dutch Song)

Hoor de wind waait door de bomen,

hier in huis zelfs waait de wind.

Zou de goede Sint wel komen,

nu hij 't weer zo lelijk vindt?

nu hij 't weer zo lelijk vindt?

Hoor wie stapt daar kinderen?

Hoor klopt daar kinderen?

Hoor wie tikt daar zachtjes tegen 't raam?

't Is een vreemdling zeker?

Die verdwaald is zeker?

Ga maar vlug eens vragen naar zijn naam!

Sint Nikolaas! Sint Nikolaas!

Breng mij vanavond ook een bezoek!

en strooi dan wat lekkers in een of d'andere hoek!

Hear How the Wind Blows

(English Translation)

Hear how the wind blows through the trees,

Even here inside the house the wind blows.

Will the good Saint come,

When the weather is that bad?

When the weather is that bad?

Listen, who's stepping there children?

Listen, who's knocking there children?

Listen, who's tapping, softly at the window?

Must be a stranger, I'm sure?

Who lost his way, I'm sure?

Quickly, go and ask his name!

Saint Nicolas! Saint Nicolas!

Please visit me too, tonight!

And throw some sweets in this or that corner!

Many thanks to Rudy Welvaert for sending us these songs.

Web Resources

You can find more kids songs from Belgium here:

www.mamalisa.com/world/belgium.html

St. Nicholas Day In France

Even though in France people generally give gifts for Christmas, there is a St. Nicholas Song they sing called La légende de Saint Nicolas. This one is about another legend of St. Nick. It's a sadder one about a butcher who slaughtered three little kids and salted them like pork. Later St. Nicholas brought them back to life.

Here's the song in French with an English translation by Monique Palomares of Mama Lisa's World en français. (www.mamalisa.com/fr).

La légende de Saint Nicolas (The Legend of St. Nicholas)

La légende de Saint Nicolas

(French Song)

Refrain:

Ils étaient trois petits enfants

Qui s'en allaient glaner aux champs.

Tant sont allés tant sont venus,

Que sur le soir se sont perdus.

S'en sont allés chez le boucher:

"Boucher voudrais-tu nous loger ?"

Refrain

"Entrez, entrez, petits enfants

Il y a d' la place assurément."

Ils n'étaient pas sitôt entrés,

Que le boucher les a tués.

Autre version

Ils n'étaient pas sitôt entrés

Que le boucher les a tués

Les a coupés en p'tits morceaux,

Mis au saloir comme pourceaux

Refrain

Saint Nicolas au bout d' sept ans

Vint à passer dedans ce champ,

Alla frapper chez le boucher:

"Boucher voudrais-tu me loger ?"

Refrain

Entrez, entrez, Saint Nicolas,

Il y a d' la place, il n'en manqu' pas."

Il n'était pas sitôt entré

Qu'il a demandé à souper.

Refrain

"Du p'tit salé je veux avoir,

Qu'il y a sept ans qu'est au saloir".

Quand le boucher entendit ça,

Hors de sa porte il s'enfuya*

Refrain

"Boucher, boucher, ne t'enfuis pas !

Repens-toi, Dieu te pardonnera".

Saint Nicolas alla s'asseoir

Dessus le bord de ce saloir

Refrain

"Petits enfants qui dormez là,

Je suis le grand Saint Nicolas."

Le grand saint étendit trois doigts,

Les p'tits se levèrent tous les trois.

Refrain

Le premier dit: "J'ai bien dormi".

Le second dit:" Et moi aussi".

A ajouté le plus petit:

"Je me croyais au paradis !"

Refrain

The Legend of Saint Nicholas

(English Translation)

Chorus

They were three little children

Who went a-gleaning in the fields.

They went so much to, so much fro

That by the evening, they got lost.

They went to the butcher's house.

"Butcher, would you accommodate us?"

Chorus

"Come in, come in, little children

There's room, for sure."

No sooner had they come in,

Then the butcher killed them.

Other version

No sooner had they come in,

Then the butcher killed them.

He cut them into small pieces,

Put them in the salting-tub as piglets.

Chorus

Saint Nicholas, after seven years,
Happened to pass in this field.
He went to knock at the butcher's door,
"Butcher, would you accommodate me?"

Chorus

"Come in, come in, Saint Nicholas.
There's room, no shortage of it".
No sooner had he come in,
Then he requested to supper.

Chorus

"I want some of the salted meat,
That's been for seven years in the salting-tub."
When the butcher heard that
He ran away from his house.

Chorus

"Butcher, butcher, don't run away!
Repent, God will forgive you".
Saint Nicholas went to sit down
On the edge of this salting-tub.

Chorus

"Little children who're sleeping there
I am the great Saint Nicholas."
The great saint stretched out three fingers.
The little ones got up, the three of them.

Chorus

The first one said "I slept well."
The second one said "And I did too."
The youngest one added:
"I thought I was in paradise!"

Chorus

Web Resources

You can listen to the tune of this song and print out the sheet music here:
http://www.mamalisa.com/?t=es&p=119&c=22

Web Resources

You can find more kids songs from France here:
http://www.mamalisa.com/world/france.html

St. Nicholas Day in Italy

Saint Nicholas Day is celebrated on December 6th in the north-east of Italy, mainly in the region that belonged to the Austro-Hungarian Empire. St. Nick is the one who brings children presents in that area, instead of Santa, Father Christmas or la Befana.

San Nicolò de Bari (Saint Nicholas of Bari)

Monique Palomares of Mama Lisa's World en français (www.mamalisa.com/fr) translated the following popular song form Veneto, in Northern Italy. The original is in a Northern Italian Dialect.

(As with many traditional songs and rhymes, some of the imagery in this song is, by modern standards, violent. We always struggle, when we're presented with material such as this, as to whether or not it is appropriate to include. In end we feel that accurately representing the cultures and traditions of the world is very important. We believe it's up to parents and educators to provide the proper context and use these problematic rhymes as a springboard for discussions about how the world has changed and progressed.)

San Nicolò de Bari

(Italian Dialect Song)

San Nicolò de Bari

Le festa dei scolari

Se i scolari no vol far festa

San Nicolò ghe taia la testa

Saint Nicholas of Bari

(English Translation)

Saint Nicholas of Bari

the children's celebration

if the children don't celebrate,

Saint Nicholas will chop their heads off.

Web Resources

You can find more kids songs from Italy here:

http://www.mamalisa.com/world/italy.html

A Personal Story About Saint Nicholas Day

Ed Gawlinski wrote...

"I also have a story about Saint Nicholas. We would give our kids little gifts on Saint Nichols Day, Saint Lucia Day, Three Kings Day, etc. Our son-in-law referred to this as the 45 days of Gawlinski Christmas... One year as Saint Nichols day approached our second child, Allison was not being well behaved. She didn't get a Saint Nicholas day present that morning. By noon, we had found where St. Nick hid the present. From then on, until well after Christmas, she was the best behaved little girl you ever saw."

Giving little gifts on the different international holidays gives you an opportunity to explain to kids how people do things differently around the world. You could also give a gift for a day of Chanukah and the Indian festival of Diwali (if you don't celebrate these holidays already).

3 - Santa Lucia's Day
December 13

About Santa Lucia's Day

Santa Lucia's Day is celebrated on December 13th in Sweden, Denmark, Norway and Finland. It commemorates the life of Santa Lucia, who is known as Saint Lucy in English.

Santa Lucia was born in Syracuse, Sicily around 283 and died in 303 AD.

The myth is that her parents wanted her to marry a man who she didn't want to marry. She wanted to devote her life to helping the poor. In protest against the marriage, she poked out her eyes and put them on a platter and sent them to the man. The legend is that her eyes were miraculously restored by God.

It's said that Saint Lucia blinded herself on the shortest, darkest day of the year, which is the Winter Solstice.

A popular saying associated with this holiday is:

Lucy Light,

The Shortest Day &

The Longest Night.

This saying celebrates the association of St Lucia's Day, December 13, with the Winter Solstice which, under the old Julian calendar, used to fall on that day. (Under the modern Calendar, the Winter Solstice falls near December 21.)

This day is very significant in Sweden and other Scandinavian countries. There, due to their very Northern geographic position, in December, the daylight time is very short and darkness and nighttime are extremely long.

Lucia is another way of saying "Lucy", which literally translates to "light". (In English we can hear this connection in words like "luminescent".) After the Winter Solstice the days get longer. So St. Lucia is a celebration of the coming lengthening of the days.

Santa Lucia's Day in Sweden (and other Scandinavian Countries)

The custom on Santa Lucia Day is for the oldest girl in the family to dress in a white robe with a red sash and wear a crown of candles and lingonberry leaves (lingonberries are popular berries in Sweden). She's supposed to be dressed as St. Lucia. The other girls dress in white with silver crowns. The boys wear pointed silver hats and carry wands with stars on them. They're called STJÄRNGOSSAR (star boys). Some kids dress up as TOMTAR which are like gnomes.

On the morning of Santa Lucia, children wake their parents and serve them a breakfast of ginger cookies, LUSSEKATTER (a special St. Lucia bun made with saffron), coffee and GLÖGG (hot spiced wine). The kids dress in their special Santa Lucia costumes and sing Santa Lucia songs.

Throughout the day girls can be seen dressed as Santa Lucia in schools, malls, churches and other public places. They sing and give out ginger cookies. There are also LUCIATAGS, St. Lucia processions in which the children dress in their white costumes and sing St. Lucia Day songs.

In Sweden, and other Scandinavian countries, Santa Lucia Day is seen as being the beginning of the Christmas season. It starts the Twelve Days of Christmas.

Natten går tunga fjät (Night Walks with a Heavy Step)

"Natten går tunga fjät" is one of the most popular carols to sing. (This song is also sometimes referred to simply as "SANKTA LUCIA.") It has a beautiful, haunting melody and it's all about the long night and the return of daylight. Here's one version of Natten går tunga fjät in Swedish, followed by an English translation.

Natten går tunga fjät

(Swedish Song)

Natten går tunga fjät
rund gård och stuva;
kring jord, som sol förlät,
skuggorna ruva.
Då i vårt mörka hus,
stiger med tända ljus,
Sankta Lucia, Sankta Lucia.

Natten går stor och stum
nu hörs dess vingar
i alla tysta rum
sus som av vingar.
Se, på vår tröskel står
vitklädd med ljus i hår
Sankta Lucia, Sankta Lucia.

Mörkret ska flykta snart
ur jordens dalar
så hon ett underbart
ord till oss talar.
Dagen ska åter ny
stiga ur rosig sky
Sankta Lucia, Sankta Lucia.

Night Walks with a Heavy Step

(English Translation)

Night walks with a heavy step
Round yard and hearth,
As the sun departs from earth,
Shadows are brooding.
There in our dark house,
Walking with lit candles,
Santa Lucia, Santa Lucia!

Night walks grand, yet silent,
Now hear its gentle wings,
In every room so hushed,
Whispering like wings.
Look, at our threshold stands,
White-clad with light in her hair,
Santa Lucia, Santa Lucia!

Darkness shall take flight soon,
From earth's valleys.
So she speaks a
Wonderful Word to us:
A new day will rise again
From the rosy sky...
Santa Lucia, Santa Lucia!

The tune to "Natten går tunga fjät" comes from an Italian version of the song called "Santa Lucia".

Web Resources

You can listen to the tune of this song and print out the sheet music here:

http://mamalisa.com/?t=es&p=1032

Sankta Lucia, skänk mig en tia (Sankta Lucia, give me a tenner)

There are at least 3 different Swedish versions of "Natten går tunga fjä".

We were told, "There are lots of alternative versions to the lyrics, the most famous being "Sankta Lucia, skänk mig en tia".

Our correspondent Lars wrote about this version:

"Hi!

I am from Sweden. The lyrics beginning with 'Sankta Lucia, skänk mig en tia' is simply an irreverent version, usually sung by kids tired of the very beautiful but also boring singing.(The fun being that it sounds exactly like the proper version.)"

The full lyrics fragment sung is as follows:

Sankta Lucia, skänk mig en tia

Inte en femma, det har jag hemma

Roughly Translated

Sankta Lucia, give me a tenner

not a fiver, I got that at home

(Note: tenner = ten crown bill, fiver = five crown bill)

Thanks Lars!

Web Resources

You can find more kids songs from Sweden here:

www.mamalisa.com/world/sweden.html

Santa Lucia in the US

Ed Gawlinki wrote...

"I had been the director of a Saint Lucia performance for over twenty years. In the American Girls' book, 'Kirsten's Surprise', Kirsten explains the Swedish Saint Lucia custom to her cousins, and they organize a Luciatag celebration. Over the years, many of the girls in my performance had a Kirsten doll, and we used these dolls in their Saint Lucia outfit or Swedish outfits to decorate our performance area. Occasionally, a girl would wear her Kirsten outfit as her costume. (Some of their mothers made costumes based on one of the outfits worn by the Kirsten American Girl doll.)"

Thanks for sharing that Ed!

4 - Saint Thomas's Day
December 21

About Saint Thomas's Day

St. Thomas's Day is named for Doubting Thomas, who was the last apostle to believe in Jesus' resurrection.

His day is on December 21st, usually the winter solstice and the darkest day of the year. St. Thomas's Day is on this day because he remained in the dark the longest.

Our correspondent, Tomas Lipps writes...

"I'm told that on St. Thomas day in Spain a turkey is traditionally cooked and served. The male turkey is, as you might know, called a tom turkey. Makes you wonder."

St. Thomas Day Nursery Rhyme 1

Here's a nursery rhyme about St. Thomas Day...

(English Nursery Rhyme)

St. Thomas Grey, St. Thomas Grey,
The longest night and the shortest day.

St. Thomas Day Nursery Rhyme 2

And here's one you can say for a couple of days after St. Thomas's Day...

(English Nursery Rhyme)

St. Thomas's day is past and gone,
And Christmas is a-most a-come,
Maidens arise
And make your pies,
And save poor tailor Bobby one.

Web Resources

For more English nursery rhymes visit:

www.mamalisa.com/house

5 - Epiphany
January 6

About Epiphany

January 6th is the Epiphany. It's the day the baptism of Christ is celebrated. (In Eastern Orthodox Churches Epiphany is celebrated on January 19, due to a difference in calendars.)

January 6th is also called Kings Day, or the Day of the Three Magi Kings or Wise Men. (Caspar, Melchior and Balthasar.) The Epiphany is celebrated in some countries as the day the three wise men visited the infant baby Jesus.

The Three Wise Men saw the star of Bethlehem on Christmas, the day Jesus was born. It took them the time between then and the Epiphany to find Jesus and present him with their gifts.

Epiphany literally means manifestation. Thus, the Epiphany is the manifestation of Christ to the Three Kings.

Kings Day (Epiphany) In France

In France, January 6th is also called La fête des rois or Kings Day.

Since the Middle Ages, in celebration of the Epiphany, French people have Galettes des Rois. Galette des Rois is called King's Cake in English. In the north of France it's a round cake with an almond/butter filling called frangipane. In the south of France, King's Cake is called a royaume and is made in the shape of a ring, representing a crown, and topped with glazed fruit and icing. Hidden inside the King's Cake is a small trinket called a fève. Whoever finds the fève is given a paper crown and gets to be king or queen for the day!

Monique Palomares of Mama Lisa's World en français (www.mamalisa.com/fr) writes...

"Friends generally gather to share a 'galette' or a 'royaume' ('kingdom' -that's the way the King's cake - a ring cake without filling -is called in Southern France). The one who finds the trinket has to buy another cake then the group gathers again and so on. We may do that at our working place too. That's why you can find cakes for sale long after January 6th."

Thanks Monique!

Web Resource

You can find a recipe for Galettes des Rois here:

http://www.mamalisa.com/blog/kings-day-in-france-and-a-recipe-for-french-kings-cake/

J'aime la galette (I Love Cake)

Here's a song called J'aime la galette, or I Love Cake, in French and with an English translation. This song is sung by kids all over France.

J'aime la galette

(French Song)

J'aime la galette,
Savez-vous comment ?
Quand elle est bien faite
Avec du beurre dedans.
Trala la la la la la lère,
Tra la la la la la la la la,
Tra la la la la la la lère,
Tra la la la la la la la.

I Love Cake

(English Translation)

I love cake,
Do you know how?
When it's well made,
With butter inside!
Tra la la la la la la la lère,
Tra la la la la la la la la,
Tra la la la la la la la lère,
Tra la la la la la la la la.

Web Resource

You can listen to the tune of this song and print out the sheet music here:

http://www.mamalisa.com/?p=782&t=es

C'est la jolie fête, la fête des Rois (It's the Pretty Day, Three Kings's Day)

Here's another French Kings Day song, sung to the tune of the popular French song "Au clair de la lune".

C'est la jolie fête, la fête des Rois

(French Song)

C'est la jolie fête
La fête des Rois
On mange la galette
Chez mon oncle Éloi
Si maman est reine
Papa sera roi
Mais si j'ai la fève
La couronne pour moi.

It's the Pretty Day, Three Kings's Day

(English Translation)

It's the pretty day,
Three Kings' day.
We eat galette
At my uncle Ray's.
If Mommy's the queen,
Daddy will be king,
But if I get the trinket,
The crown is for me.

Web Resource

You can listen to the tune of this song and print out the sheet music here:

http://www.mamalisa.com/?t=es&p=3006

Web Resource

You can find more songs from France here:

http://www.mamalisa.com/world/france.html

Kings Day (Epiphany) In The United States

The tradition of eating King's Cake is also followed in New Orleans in the U.S. (Many people of French descent, called Cajuns, live in that area.) There, King's cake is a ring cake made with cinnamon dough and topped with icing. The icing is purple for justice, green for faith and gold for power.

King's Cake is eaten in New Orleans throughout the Mardi Gras season, which begins on the Epiphany. A small baby, representing Jesus, is hidden inside the New Orleans version of King's Cake. Whoever finds the baby is supposed to have good luck.

Web Resource

You can find more Cajun songs here:

http://www.mamalisa.com/world/cajun.html

The Epiphany in Spanish Speaking Cultures

The Epiphany is especially important in Spain and other Spanish speaking cultures around the world, where the day is called Fiesta de Los Tres Reyes Magos (Three Kings Day Celebration).

In Spain, Three Kings Day is celebrated like Christmas. It's the day the children are given presents. On the night of the 5th, instead of stockings, kids leave their shoes out, stuffed with straw. It's not Santa who comes in the middle of the night leaving the children presents. Instead, it's the three magi who come bringing gifts for the kids, just like they gave the baby Jesus presents in honor of his birth. The straw in the children's shoes is for the Wise Men's camels to eat.

To celebrate the Epiphany in Spain there are also often parades featuring the three magi.

The special food that is eaten on the Epiphany is called Roscón de Reyes, meaning "twisted roll of kings". It's a loaf in the shape of a crown with fruit and nuts on top and filled with chocolate or whipped cream. There's supposed to be a gold coin inside it. It's said that the person who finds the coin will have good luck throughout the upcoming year.

Our correspondent, who writes as "Ladyowner", tells us...

"Greetings from Spain!!!! Today is a really important day for children and adults alike...the 3 wise men are coming so everybody is thrilled waiting for their gifts...It doesn't matter if you are a Catholic or not. Everybody follows this tradition that is complimented with a traditional parade in every single city/village of Spain in which the three wise men throw candies to the kids riding their camels, horses or in fancy chariots!!!"

Thanks Ladyowner!

Web Resource

For songs in the Spanish Language visit:

http://www.mamalisa.com/?lang=Spanish&t=el

La Befana and the Epiphany in Italy

"Befana" is Italian for "Epiphany". It's also the name of a character from an interesting legend that strongly influenced the Italian traditions for celebrating this holiday.

On their way to deliver gifts to the baby Jesus, the Three Wise Men came across a woman named Befana. They asked her to come with them, but she refused, saying she had too much housework to do. Later she realized she had made a mistake. She ran off with her broom in search of the Magi, bearing her own presents for the baby Jesus. But she never caught up to them. It's said that Befana is still searching for the baby Jesus.

In Italy, it's Befana, and not Santa Claus, who goes around giving gifts to all the children, in imitation of the Three Wise men bringing gifts to Jesus.

Befana looks like a friendly witch, in tattered clothes and with a mole on her face. She flies on a broom and goes down the chimneys to deliver gifts to all the children.

Families leave out a tangerine or an orange and a glass of wine for La Befana. She consumes it all and leaves behind a handprint of ashes on the plate (that she got while coming down the fireplace).

Our correspondent, Maria Sabatino-Cabardo writes...

"In my dad's family, each child got oranges, nuts, a small toy (sometimes) and also a small lump of coal. Nonno said it was to remind them to be good! or else... Thanks for a great site, you have found a lot of songs I almost forgot from my childhood. And lets keep up the Italian traditions, in fact, all our mother countries traditions."

Thanks Maria!

La Befana vien di notte (The Befana Comes at Night)

Here's a nursery song children chant in Italy for La Befana.

La Befana vien di notte

(Italian Nursery Rhyme)

La Befana vien di notte
con le scarpe tutte rotte
col cappello alla romana
viva viva la Befana!

The Befana Comes at Night

(English Translation)

The Befana comes at night
In worn out shoes
Dressed like a Roman
Long live the Befana!

Our correspondent Maria Sabatino-Cabardo writes:

"Hi and Grazie for this song.

My mom who is from Italy used to sing this to us all the time and she has now taught my 4 year old and 2 year old this legend and song but she sings a slightly different song:

La Befana vien di notte
con le scarpe tutte rotte
ai bambini piccolini lascie tanti ciocolatini
ai bambini cativoni lascie cenere e carbone

Excuse my spelling it may not be correct but it is the song they sing in Roseto Valfortore, a little mountain town in Puglia.

The english would be:

The Befana comes at night
In worn out shoes
To the little children she leaves a lot of little chocolates
To the bad little children she leaves ashes and coal

You know this is a great legend and I hope all Italians and those of Italian origin keep up the legend and teach this to our children."

Thanks Maria!

Web Resource

For songs from Italy visit:

http://www.mamalisa.com/world/italy.html

6 - Saint Knut's Day
January 13

About Saint Knut's Day

St. Knut's Day is a holiday celebrated in Sweden, Finland and Norway, on January 13th. The day is called Tjugondag Knut in Sweden, which means Knut's 20th day. In Norway it's called Tyvendedagen, which is the 20th day. That's because St. Knut's Day is 20 days from Christmas.

On St. Knut's Day, the Christmas tree is "plundered". If there are edible ornaments on the tree, they'll be eaten. If there weren't any on the tree, sometimes new ones will be placed there for the kids to take off and eat. It's an incentive to take off all the other decorations and get rid of the tree.

Then kids dance around the tree singing.

In Sweden they sing...

TJUGONDAG KNUT DANSAS JULEN UT. (Swedish)

KNUT'S 20TH DAY (ST. KNUT'S DAY) DANCES CHRISTMAS AWAY.(English)

Sometimes it'll be longer...

PÅ TJUGONDAG KNUT DANSAS JULEN UT OCH DÅ PLUNDRAS OCH KASSERAS GRANEN. (Swedish)

AT ST. KNUT'S DAY, DANCE CHRISTMAS AWAY AND THEN PLUNDER AND SCRAP THE SPRUCE TREE. (English)

After which, they either throw out the tree, or chop it up and use it as fire wood.

In Norway, they say a similar rhyme:

SANTE KNUT OG JAGA JULA UT. (Norwegian)

ST. KNUT CHASES CHRISTMAS AWAY. (English)

Sometimes there are also carnivals for St. Knut's day.

A little history behind the holiday...

King Canute (circa 994 – 1035) was a Viking who was also known as Knut and Knud. He was king of England, Denmark, and for a while Norway and part of Sweden.

Early on, when he took over England, he was merciless to prisoners, he cut off their noses, ears and hands. Later, he repented for what he had done. To make up for his cruelty, he joined the church and tried to create peace and justice in his land. Under his rule, there was peace for 18 years. (Although, he may have been responsible for some political murders.)

One of the laws he made, while he was king, was that the Christmas season would last 20 days, and that no one should fast during that time. Thus the holiday season would end on January 13th. That's the day that's come to be known as St. Knut's Day.

Our correspondent, Bonnie C. Schnars, writes...

"I was interested in the history of this holiday as my family celebrates it in the United States. I had great aunts whose parents came from Sweden. We traditionally decorate a small tree on this day, the kids in the family sit on the table and decorate the tree and when this is accomplished we dance around the tree holding hands and singing. After this is completed our family sits around the living room and Santa hides a box of presents for the family. Each person gets a gift. There is a twist, to get your present first poems are read about each person, everyone has to guess who the poem is about, then the person gets their gift. We have a big dinner and basically hang out with the family. We are one of the only families from this area that celebrates this. It is nice to know the history now."

Kristina writes...

"Knut was/is a rather festive day. At least up until 50 years ago. Children liked it a lot as the tree was often decorated with candy (candy canes, sugar decorations and smällkarameller/crackers with hidden bits of candy). All christmas they had to look at these sweets without eating it, but on Knut all decorations were taken down and the candy could be eaten. That is called julgransplundring (christmas tree looting).

As we no longer have much candy in the trees and few people want to eat old candy, it's not as big as it used to be. Some still see it as a festive day and invite kids over for a kids party were they hand out candy. There are also some different local traditions."

Nu är glada julen slut, slut, slut. (Now the merry Christmas is over, over, over)

Kristina also contributed the following St. Knut's Day song...

Nu är glada julen slut, slut, slut.

(Swedish Song)

Nu är glada julen slut, slut, slut.
Julegranen bäres ut, ut, ut.

Men till nästa jul igen,
kommer han vår gamle vän,
för det har han lovat.

Now the merry Christmas is over, over, over

(English Translation)

Now the merry Christmas is over, over, over,
The Christmas tree is carried out, out, out,
But for next Christmas again,
He is coming our old friend
Because he has promised that.

Thanks Kristina!

Web Resources

You can find more kids songs from Sweden here:

www.mamalisa.com/world/sweden.html

7 - Part 2
Christmas Songs and Traditions From Around The World

8 - Tu scendi dalle stelle
(You Come Down From The Stars)
Italian Song

About Tu scendi dalle stelle

Many people grew up hearing this lovely Italian song at Christmastime. After we originally posted it on our blog, we were amazed by the amount of people who wrote in saying how much this song touched them.

It was originally composed in 1754 in Nola by Saint Alfonso Maria de' Liguori, a Neapolitan bishop, and published the next year. The lyrics were first written in Neapolitan dialect. "Quanno nascette Ninno" means "When Baby (Jesus) was born". The song was later re-written in standard Italian by pope Pius IX.

Tu scendi dalle stelle (You come down from the stars)

Tu scendi dalle stelle

(Italian Song)

Tu scendi dalle stelle
O Re del Cielo
E vieni in una grotta
Al freddo al gelo.

E vieni in una grotta
Al freddo al gelo.

O Bambino mio Divino
Io ti vedo qui a tremar,
O Dio Beato
Ah, quanto ti costò
L'avermi amato.
Ah, quanto ti costò
L'avermi amato.

A te che sei del mondo,
Il creatore
Mancano panni e fuoco,
O mio Signore.
Mancano panni e fuoco,
O mio Signore.

Caro eletto, Pargoletto,
Quanto questa povertà,
Piu m'innamora
Giacche ti fece amor
Povero ancora.
Giacche ti fece amor
Povero ancora.

You Come Down from the Stars

(English Translation)

You come down from the stars
Oh King of Heavens,
And you come in a cave
In the cold, in the frost.
And you come in a cave
In the cold, in the frost.

Oh my Divine Baby
I see you trembling here,
Oh Blessed God
Ah, how much it cost you,
Your loving me.
Ah, how much it cost you,
Your loving me.

For you, who are of all the world
The creator,
No robes and fire,
Oh my Lord,
No robes and fire,
Oh my Lord.

Dear chosen one, little infant,
This dire poverty,
Makes me love you more.
Since Love made you
Poor now.
Since Love made you
Poor now.

Web Resources

You can listen to the tune of this song and find sheet music here:

http://www.mamalisa.com/?t=es&p=1313&c=120

You can watch video performances of this song here:

http://www.mamalisa.com//blog/?p=617

A Sampling of our correspondence about Tu scendi dalle stelle

Eugene Giudice wrote...

"The song Tu scendi dalle stelle takes me back to my youth when as schoolchilren, we would go at Christmas time to the Villa Scalabrini, which is an Italian nursing home and sing this song to the residents."

Marti Bryant wrote...

"This song means so much to my aunt, mom and me. My grandmother sang this to my aunt and mom when they were little girls and me to when I was a little girl."

Elizabeth wrote...

"My Mom would sing part of this song. Her father sang it to his eight daughters but passed away before they could learn all the words. I lost my Mom last year. Now I can teach my children and grandchildren and we will have still another memory of our special angel."

Dominic Tortelli wrote...

"This has been a long standing tradition in my family to either listen to a recording or sing the song ourselves on Christmas. I was in the 4th grade when I learned this song and sang it at midnight mass.

At St. Rocco church in Cleveland, Ohio tu scendi... has been sung at midnight mass for the past 83 years."

Piera Gamble wrote...

"Thank you so much for 'Tu scendi dalle stelle' my mom is in a nursing home with dementia. We were trying to sing the song and we did not know the words. Now it will be fun for me to learn and sing with my dear mom."

Terrie Ledwich wrote...

"I thank you for printing the lyrics to this song. My parish (St. Anthony of Padua, now St. Clare of Assisi) used to sing this song every Christmas Eve at the beginning of Midnight Mass. The priest would come in the procession with a little child from the parish, who would be carrying the baby Jesus. When they got to the manger, he would put the Bambino in the manger as everyone sang the song. It was very beautiful. With the lyrics and sheet music from this site, I am hoping that our priest will agree to revive that old tradition in our parish this year!"

Martha Parisi wrote...

"This beautiful song is the original Italian verson. It has been re-recorded many times in an English version (not a literal translation) under the name O' Bambino. The best known being that of the Harry Simeone Chorale called 'O Bambino' (One Cold and Blessed Winter). It is also very beautiful. As kids, my parents played it on a 33rpm record, titled 'The Little Drummer Boy', which I still have. Then I purchased it on a cassette and subsequently a CD released by MCA Records-Special Products Division. The copyright is 1971 MCA Records, Inc., Universal City, California 91608–USA Distributed by UNI Distribution, Corp. I have seen it every year in major department stores under the same 'Harry Simeone Chorale–The Little Drummer Boy' title!

As far as the original Italian version goes, my absolute favorite version is sung by Luciano Pavorotti!! It is divine as, to me, it is the closest sound to heaven-here on earth! His recordings of it can be found in so many numerous offerings; too many to list here !!! I am almost certain that it is on my Andrea Bocelli CD's also."

Frank La Mantia wrote...

"I remember singing Tu Scendi Dalle Stelle with friend when living in Palermo Sicily, we walked around the town and celebrated Christmas with neighbors and accepted freshly baked Sicilian Biscotti, that was a fun time for me."

Patricia Volante wrote...

"I live in England, but this Christmas song has wonderful memories for me of Christmas spent in a small village called Valvori in Lazio, while visiting relatives there. The little church full for midnight mass and the heat from hundreds of candles keeping us warm in the front row. We sang this song then, and also when we visited the many presepe, accompanied by the sound of the piffero and the zampogna. Wonderful!"

Synchopepper wrote...

'I have performed this carol for the last few years and in my research have found some interesting things about it.

It appears to have originated in northern Italy tradition when in the distant past shepherds descended to small hill towns to form musical processions singing and accompanying the songs with the piffero and the zampogna. It was known as the Bagpipers Carol.

In addition to many beautiful Italian versions recorded, Paddy Maloney of the Irish musical group 'The Cheiftains' made a beautiful Christmas recording a few years back in which he used this theme as an overture. Also American folksinger Pete Seeger created English lyrics based on what he thought the original shepherds would have expressed."

Toni Lockhart wrote...

"My father grew up in the tiny village of Torrecuso Italy. He tells me that when he was a child the bagpipers would walk through the town playing this song at Christmas. I think he called them the Zampugnara (not sure of the spelling)..."

Thanks to everyone who wrote to us about this beautiful song!

Web Resources

You can find many more Italian kid songs here:

http://www.mamalisa.com/world/italy.html

9 - Tomtarnas Julnatt
(The Gnomes' Christmas Night)
Swedish Song

About Tomtarnas Julnatt

Our correspondent, Leif Stensson from Project Runeberg (http://runeberg.org), wrote me about an old tradition in Sweden relating to Gnomes. He also sent me the song THE GNOMES' CHRISTMAS NIGHT in Swedish and with an English translation.

Leif wrote...

"Here is a children's song and Christmas song which draws on the old folk superstition about 'tomtar' (singular 'tomte'), a kind of tiny, benevolent elf or gnome that liked to take up residence near or under houses that were close to a forest, and tended to be occasionally useful to the inhabitants of the house if they treated it well. Typically, they would help lost sheep find their way home, and the like. Tomtar presumably lived off nuts and berries, but in the winter when these were hard to find, it was customary to set out a bowl of porridge outside the front door late in the evening, so that the local tomte had something to eat. Especially around Christmas.

On Christmas Eve, it was customary in remote farms to set the dining table for a feast, and leave it overnight. The local tomte as well as ones from neighbouring houses and from the forest would then sneak in and eat whatever they wanted during the night, and then the people of the house would eat the next day. This song is about a gang of tomtar visiting on a Christmas night. Every verse ends with the nonsense sequence 'tipp, tapp, tipp, tapp, tippetippetipp tapp! Tipp, tipp, tapp', the sound of small feet tiptoeing around. I've left it out of the text below."

Note: Leif was kind enough to provide annotations to this song, which we present after the English translation.

Tomtarnas Julnatt (The Gnomes' Christmas Night)

Tomtarnas Julnatt

(Swedish Song)

Midnatt råder,
tyst det är i husen,
tyst i husen.
Alla sover,
släckta äro ljusen,
äro ljusen.

Se, då krypa
tomtar upp ur vrårna
upp ur vrårna,
lyssna, speja,
trippa fram på tårna,
fram på tårna.

Snälla folket
låtit maten rara,
maten rara,
stå på bordet
åt en tomteskara,
tomteskara.

Hur de mysa,
hoppa upp bland faten,
upp bland faten,
tissla, tassla*,
"God är julematen,
julematen!"

Gröt och skinka,
lilla äppelbiten,
äppelbiten,
tänk så rart
det smakar Nisse** liten,
Nisse liten.

Nu till lekar!
Glada skratten klingar,
skratten klingar,
runt om granen***
skaran muntert svingar,
muntert svingar.

Natten lider.
Snart de tomtar snälla,
tomtar snälla,
kvick och näpet
allt i ordning ställa,
ordning ställa.

Sedan åter
in i tysta vrårna,
tysta vrårna,
tomteskaran
tassar lätt på tårna,
lätt på tårna.

The Gnomes' Christmas Night

(English Translation)

Midnight reigns,
it's quiet in the houses,
quiet in the houses.
Everyone sleeps,
the candles are put out,
candles put out.

Look, there comes
the gnomes out from the corners,
from the corners,
list'ning, watching,
sneaking on their toes,
on their toes.

The nice people
have left the sweet food,
the sweet food,
on the table
for a band of gnomes,
band of gnomes.

How they frolic,
skipping between dishes,
between dishes,
whisper, murmur*
"It's good, the Christmas food,
Christmas food."

Porridge, ham,
the little piece of apple,
piece of apple,
ah how sweet
it tastes for little Gnomie**,
little Gnomie**.

Now the games!
Happy laughter sounding,
laughter sounding,
'round the tree***
the gang merrily swings,
merrily swings.

Night is ending.
Soon the friendly gnomes,
friendly gnomes,
quickly, neatly,
putting all in order,
all in order.

Then, back
into the quiet corners,
quiet corners,
the gang of gnomes
sneak on their toes,
on their toes.

Annotations to *The Gnomes Christmas Night*

* The Swedish words "tissla" and "tassla" are not exactly real words, but rather both onomatopoetic slang for whisper, murmur, with a suggestion of secrecy, connivance, urgency, or delight.

** "Nisse" is the standard nickname for someone whose name is "Nils", but also a variation on "tomte". (The word "nisse", however, was also used for a faerytale creature similar to the "tomte", but who was not necessarily benevolent. Perhaps somewhat like the Irish-style leprechaun.) In this instance, "Nisse" is used as a substitute for the nisse's real name, which is not known. Names were magical in the old superstition, and supernatural creatures in particular were generally unwilling to reveal their real names. In the case of this song, it is hard to say if "Nisse" is used deliberately in keeping with this superstition, or just happened to be the writer's convenient way of naming a nisse. "Gnomie" is a mediocre compromise between these possibilities.

*** In cases when the room was large enough to allow it, dancing in a circle around the Christmas tree, singing songs like this one, was a traditional Christmas game for children. In more modern tradition, this practice still lives at larger Christmas parties for children, typically in elementary schools, the little leagues of various sports, etc, after eating but before distributing presents.

WE'RE GRATEFUL TO LEIF STENSSON OF PROJECT RUNEBERG, FOR SENDING US TOMTARNAS JULNATT – THE GNOMES' CHRISTMAS NIGHT WITH SUCH INTERESTING COMMENTARY. TACK SÅ MYCKET!

Project Runeberg (http://runeberg.org) IS AN OPEN, VOLUNTARY PROJECT WHOSE PURPOSE IS TO MAKE CLASSIC NORDIC LITERATURE AND ART AVAILABLE IN ELECTRONIC FORM TO THE PUBLIC, FREE OF CHARGE.

Web Resources

You can find more kids songs from Sweden here:

www.mamalisa.com/world/sweden.html

10 - Traditions: Colombia

Christmas in Colombia

Christmas in Colombia is Like a Big Block Party!

Really! For all of you who live in the northern hemisphere – remember that Christmas in Colombia occurs at the beginning of summer. Starting around December 23rd and lasting through the night of the 25th a big party is held.

People close off their streets to traffic – they don't need permits because everyone knows it's what you do at Christmastime. They take out their stereos and dance all night.

The traditional food for this party is pork. Colombians will roast a whole pig on a spit over a barbeque.

If you're going to Colombia at this time of year, expect a big party and loud noise to last throughout the night.

And yes! Santa does visit Colombia for Christmas as do the Three Wise Men for the Epiphany on January 6th.

Our correspondent, Bill Todd, writes...

"*I would agree with you on everything except 'Christmas in Colombia occurs at the beginning of summer'. It does not. Colombia lies at the equator but the part where most people would be traveling for vacation is in the northern hemisphere. It would still be the beginning of winter, but the Colombians don't view things this way. The climate is what I would call 'vertical' as opposed to 'seasonal' ala the USA. In Cartagena on the coast it is nearly always hot and in the Bogota in the mountains it is nearly always cool to cold. This is the case all year round. To change your climate, change your altitude. Places are referred to as being 'hot' or 'cold' depending on their local environment which varies little over the course of a year.*

The term 'invierno', literally 'winter' is used more to describe periods of cooler weather associated with rainy spells. These may occur at times other than December through March.

Whatever the season, location or climate, you can count on parties, and Christmas is special."

Thanks Bill!

11 - Good King Wenceslas
English Carol

About Good King Wenceslas

Good King Wenceslas was written in 1853 by the Englishman John Mason Neale. The tune is from "Tempus Adest Floridum", a spring carol from the 13th Century.

GOOD KING WENCESLAS has become a Christmas song, even though it sings about St. Stephen's Day, which is the day after Christmas.

Wenceslas was born in 907. He was actually the Duke of Bohemia, not a king. Bohemia is now an area of the Czech Republic.

The story of "King" Wenceslas is a sad one. When he was 13 his father was killed in battle. His mother, Drahomira, became the ruler of Bohemia. She seems to have been a pagan. His grandmother taught Wenceslas Christian ideals. His mother was threatened by this and had his grandmother killed. Two years later she was deposed in an uprising and King Wenceslas became the ruler of Bohemia. He was said to be an honest, kind man. He even allowed his mother to move back into the castle with him. Unfortunately, his evil brother Boleslav murdered him in 929.

King Wenceslas eventually became a saint.

Good King Wenceslas

(English Song)

Good King Wenceslas looked out
On the feast of Stephen
When the snow lay round about
Deep and crisp and even
Brightly shone the moon that night
Though the frost was cruel
When a poor man came in sight
Gathering winter fuel.

"Hither, page, and stand by me
If you know it, telling
Yonder peasant, who is he?
Where and what his dwelling?"
"Sire, he lives a good league hence
Underneath the mountain
Right against the forest fence
By Saint Agnes' fountain."

"Bring me flesh and bring me wine
Bring me pine logs hither
You and I will see him dine
When we bear him thither."
Page and monarch forth they went
Forth they went together
Through the rude wind's wild lament
And the bitter weather.

"Sire, the night is darker now
And the wind blows stronger
Fails my heart, I know not how,
I can go no longer."
"Mark my footsteps, my good page
Tread you in them boldly
You shall find the winter's rage
Freeze your blood less coldly."

In his master's steps he trod
Where the snow lay dinted
Heat was in the very sod
Which the Saint had printed
Therefore, Christian men, be sure
Wealth or rank possessing
You who now will bless the poor
Shall yourselves find blessing.

Web Resources

You can listen to the tune of this song and print out the sheet music here:

http://www.mamalisa.com/blog/?p=112

12 - Patapan
(Willie Take Your Little Drum)
French Song

About Patapan

PATAPAN, or GUILLAUME PRENDS TON TAMBOURIN, is a traditional song from the Burgundy region in France. It's also known in English as WILLIE TAKE YOUR LITTLE DRUM. It was written by Bernard de la Monnoye (1641-1728) around 1700. Monnoye wrote many other Burgundian carols around the same time.

A tambourin is a small cylindrical drum, usually made out of wood and covered with an animal skin. It's hung from the shoulders and played with the hands. 'Turelurelu' is the sound the flute makes and 'patapatapan' is the sound of the drum. This is most likely the inspiration for the English Christmas song, THE LITTLE DRUMMER BOY.

Patapan (Willie Take Your Little Drum)

Patapan

(French Song)

Guillaume prends ton tambourin
Toi, prends ta flûte, Robin;
Au son de ces instruments
Turelurelu, patapatapan
Au son de ces instruments
Je dirai Noël gaîment.

C'était la mode autrefois
De louer le Roi des rois
Au son de ces instruments
Turelurelu, patapatapan
Au son de ces instruments
Il nous en faut faire autant.

L'homme et Dieu sont plus d'accord
Que la flûte et le tambour;
Au son de ces instruments
Turelurelu, patapatapan
Au son de ces instruments
Chantons, dansons, sautons en!

Willie take your little drum

(English Translation)

Here's a fairly literal English translation....

Willie take your little drum,
Robin take your flute, come!
To the sound of these instruments
Tu-re-lu-re-lu, pat-a-pat-a-pan,
To the sound of these instruments
I will joyfully sing Merry Christmas!

It was the way of yonder times
To praise the king of kings
To the sound of these instruments
Tu-re-lu-re-lu, pat-a-pat-a-pan,
To the sound of these instruments
We must do the same.

Man and god agree
About the flute and the little drum...
To the sound of these instruments
Tu-re-lu-re-lu, pat-a-pat-a-pan,
To the sound of these instruments
Sing! Dance! Jump around!

Guillô, pran ton tamborin

(Burgundian Dialect)

Here's Patapan in the old Burgundian dialect, which has an additional verse (#3)...

Guillô, pran ton tamborin;
Toi, pran tai fleúte, Rôbin!
Au son de cé instruman,
Turelurelu, patapatapan,
Au son de cé instruman
Je diron Noei gaiman

C' étó lai môde autrefoi
De loüé le Roi dé Roi,
Au son de cés instruman,
Turelurelu, patapatapan,
Au son de cés instruman,
Ai nos an fau faire autan.

Ce jor le Diale at ai cu
Randons an graice ai Jesu
Au son de cés instruman,
Turelurelu, patapatapan,
Au son de cés instruman,
Fezon lai nique ai Satan.

L'homme et Dei son pu d'aicor
Que lai fleúte & le tambor.
Au son de cés instruman,
Turelurelu, patapatapan,
Au son de cés instruman,
Chanton, danson, sautons-an.

Web Resources

You can find a link to a recording of this song here:

http://www.mamalisa.com/blog/?p=120

Web Resources

You can find more kids songs from France here:

http://www.mamalisa.com/world/france.html

13 - Huachí toritó
(Giddy-up, Little Bull)
Bolivian Song

Huachí toritó (Giddy-up, Little Bull)

Huachí toritó

(Bolivian Song in Spanish)

Que le daremos al niño bonito.
Que le daremos que no le haga mal,
le daremos una cesta de guindas
para que coma y pueda jugar.

Al huachí, huachi toritó
toritó del corralitó
Al huachí, huachi toritó
toritó del corralitó.

Al niñó recién nacido
todos le ofrecen un don,
yo soy pobre, nada tengo
le ofrezco mi corazón.

Huachitó, toritó
toritó del corralitó
Huachitó, toritó
toritó del corralitó.

San José y María
y Santa Isabel
vagan por las calles
de Jerusalén.

Preguntando a todos
del niño Jesús
Todos les responden
que ha muerto en la cruz.
Todos les responden
que ha muerto en la cruz.

Al huachí, huachi toritó
toritó del corralitó
Al huachí, huachi toritó
toritó del corralitó.

Giddy-up, Little Bull

(English Translation)

What will we give to the nice baby.
What will we give that'd do him no harm,
We'll give him a basket of Morillo cherries
So he can eat and play.

Giddy-up! Giddy-up, little bull,
Little bull from the little farm.
Giddy-up! Giddy-up, little bull,
Little bull from the little farm.

To the new-born baby
They all give a present.
I am poor, I have nothing,
I give him my heart.

Giddy-up, little bull,
Little bull from the little farm.
Giddy-up, little bull,
Little bull from the little farm.

Saint Joseph and Mary
And Saint Elizabeth
Are roaming in the streets
Of Jerusalem.

They're asking everybody for
News of the infant Jesus.
All of them answer
He died on the cross.
All of them answer
He died on the cross.

Giddy-up! Giddy-up, little bull,
Little bull from the little farmyard.
Giddy-up! Giddy-up, little bull,
Little bull from the little farmyard.

Many thanks to Susana Mariscal, Daniel Dorado and Joaquin Dorado for contributing this song. ¡Muchas gracias!

Web Resources

You can find more kids songs from Bolivia here:

http://www.mamalisa.com/world/bolivia.html

14 - Traditions:
Holly

The Tradition of Decorating with Holly

Holly is used to decorate houses at Christmas time and is a symbol of the season. Like many symbols, its roots can be traced to older celebrations.

Holly was used in the time of the Romans in the Saturnalia. This was a festival devoted to Saturn, the god of the harvest. It was a time of much merry making, taking place on December 17th. The Romans decorated their homes with holly and other evergreens. It was supposed to symbolize good luck.

For Christians, Holly also symbolizes Jesus Christ's crown of thorns. That's because its leaves are spiky and the berries symbolize his blood.

But Give Me Holly, Bold and Jolly

Here's a poem by Christina Rossetti (1830-1894), about holly and other plants…

But Give Me Holly, Bold and Jolly

English Poem

A ROSE has thorns as well as honey,
I'll not have her for love or money;
An iris grows so straight and fine
That she shall be no friend of mine;
Snowdrops like the snow would chill me;
Nightshade would caress and kill me;
Crocus like a spear would fright me;
Dragon's-mouth might bark or bite me;
Convolvulus but blooms to die;
A wind-flower suggests a sigh;
Love-lies-bleeding makes me sad;
And poppy-juice would drive me mad: –
But give me holly, bold and jolly,
Honest, prickly, shining holly;
Pluck me holly leaf and berry
For the day when I make merry.

15 - Fum, Fum, Fum
(Twenty-Fifth of December)
Spanish and Catalan Song

About Fum, Fum, Fum

FUM, FUM, FUM or VEINTICINCO DE DICIEMBRE, is a very popular Christmas Carol throughout the Spanish speaking world. There are different versions, but from what I can tell, this is one of the more common ones.

This carol has its roots in a Catalan Christmas Carol called A vint-i-cinq de desembre or Fum, Fum, Fum.

It seems that "Fum, fum, fum" is imitating either the sound of strumming on a guitar or the beating on a drum. (On the other hand, our correspondent Afra writes *"In fact, 'fum fum fum' means 'smoke smoke smoke'. I suppose that's because in Catalunya, in december is when people make a fire and sit next to it to sing and talk."*)

Here's the Spanish version of Fum, Fum, Fum, with an English translation, followed by the Catalan version, with an English translation.

Fum, Fum, Fum

Fum, Fum, Fum

(Spanish Song)

Veinticinco de Diciembre,
fum, fum, fum.
Veinticinco de Diciembre,
fum, fum, fum.

Como un sol nació Jesús,
radiando luz, radiando luz.
De María era hijo;
un establo fue su cuna,
fum, fum, fum.

Veinticinco de Diciembre,
fum, fum, fum.
Veinticinco de Diciembre,
fum, fum, fum.

Como un sol nació Jesús,
radiando luz, radiando luz.
De María era hijo;
un establo fue su cuna,
fum, fum, fum.

Fum, Fum, Fum

(English Translation)

Twenty-fifth of December,
Fum, fum, fum.
Twenty-fifth of December,
Fum, fum, fum.

Like a sun, was born Jesus,
Radiating light, radiating light.

He was son of Maria;
A stable was his cradle,
Fum, fum, fum.

Twenty-fifth of December,
Fum, fum, fum.
Twenty-fifth of December,
Fum, fum, fum.

Like a sun, was born Jesus,
Radiating light, radiating light.
He was son of Maria;
A stable was his cradle,
Fum, fum, fum.

Web Resources

You can listen to the tune of this song and see a video of a performance here:

http://www.mamalisa.com/?t=es&p=620&c=71

Web Resources

You can find many more Spanish kid songs here:

http://www.mamalisa.com/?t=el&lang=spanish

A vint-i-cinq de desembre (On the Twenty-fifth of December)

A vint-i-cinq de desembre

(Catalan Song)

This Catalan Carol is thought to have been written in the 16th or 17th century.

A vint-i-cinq de desembre
Fum, fum, fum
A nascut un minyonet
Ros i blanquet, ros i blanquet
Fill de la Verge Maria
N'és nat en una establia
Fum fum fum.

Aquí a dalt de la muntanya
Fum, fum, fum
Si n'hi ha dos pastorets
Abrigadets, abrigadets
Amb la pell i la samarra
Mengen ous i botifara.
Fum, fum, fum

Nit enllà el sol desperta
Fum, fum, fum
Veuen l'angel resplendent
Que els va dient :
Ara es nat a l'establia
Deu infant fill de Maria
Fum, fum, fum

A vint-i-cinc de desembre
Fum, fum, fum
És el dia de Nadal
Molt principal
En sortint de les Maitines
Menjarem cosetas finas
Fum, fum, fum

Déu nos dó unes santes festes
Fum, fum, fum
Faci fred faci calor
Serà el millor, serà el millor
De Jesús fem gran memòria
Perqué ens vulgui dar la Glòria
Fum, fum, fum

On the Twenty-fifth of December

(English Translation)

On the twenty-fifth of December
Fum, fum, fum
A little baby was born
Blond and pale
Son of Virgin Mary
Was born in a cowshed
Fum, fum fum

There, at the top of the mountain
Fum, fum, fum
There are two little shepherds
Well bundled up, well bundled up
In a skin and a cloak
They're eating eggs and sausage
Fum fum fum

Overnight, the sun goes out
Fum fum fum
They see the glowing angel
Who tells them:
Now was born, in a cowshed
The Infant God, son of Mary
Fum, fum, fum

On the twenty-fifth of December
Fum fum fum
Is Christmas day
Very important
When morning mass is over
We'll eat very nice food
Fum fum fum

May God give us some holy celebrations
Fum fum fum
Be it cold, be it hot
It'll be best, it'll be best
Let's make Jesus a great celebration
So he'll want to give us Glory
Fum fum fum

Our correspondent Ted Figlock writes...

"This carol was reported to be a favorite of St. Ignatius Loyola, a Basque. Isn't it nice to imagine him, the founder of the Society of Jesus (Jesuits), usually pictured as a pretty stern looking character, enjoying Christmastime and singing carols? And it is yours to enjoy, too."

Thanks Ted!

Web Resources

You can listen to a recording of this song here:

http://www.mamalisa.com/?t=es&p=622&c=45

Web Resources

You can find more kids songs from Catalan here:

http://www.mamalisa.com/world/catalan.html

16 - Traditions: Occitan

Christmas in Occitan

Occitania is a region of southern France, and parts of Spain and Italy, where the Occitan language used to be the primary tongue.

Occitan, also called "Langue d'oc" (literally "Language of Yes") still survives as a language.

It was the language of the medieval Troubadours and the Nobel Prize winning poet Frederic Mistral.

The word Occitan also refers to the culture of the area.

Hugues Bernet is a teacher in a school in France where the Occitan language and culture are taught.

Hugues wrote to me about a custom they follow in his school at Christmastime. It involves a recitation in Occitan. Here's what he wrote:

Here is a small Occitan custom that's practiced at Christmastime. I don't know it's date or precise origin (the term "cachafuoc" for "Yule log" comes from the Cévennes mountains in south central France). Nonetheless, in the school where I work, we organize a little party for Christmas where we recapture this custom.

During this party the gifts are given out to all the people there. That's the "soca" (a log) that brings the gifts. Two people (the youngest and the oldest of the group) carry the log into the room and say a ritual phrase in Occitan:

Bota fuòc, cachafuòc,
que nos alegre,
que nos fague la jòia d'èstre aquíi l'an que ven,
e se sèm pas mai,
que siaguem pas mens!

English Translation:

Light up, Yule log,
Delight us,
Give us the joy to be here next year,
And if we aren't more numerous,
Let us not be less!

Many thanks to Hugues for sharing this nice saying and custom with us!

17 - Nadal Tindaire (Jingling Christmas) Occitan Song

Nadal Tindaire (Jingling Christmas)

Monique Palomares of Mama Lisa's World en français (www.mamalisa.com/fr) sent us the lyrics and English translation of NADAL TINDAIRE *an Occitan Christmas song.*

Nadal Tindaire

(Occitan Song)

Avèm ausit las aubadas
Que se'n venon de sonar
Sus de trompetas dauradas
Dison qu'un Daufin serà
L'una fa :"Tarara tararèra
Lintampon ladèri tampon"
E l'autra li fa lo respon :
"Tarara tararèra
Lintampon ladèri tampon"
Novèl vengut pichon popon

Quand dintrarem dins l'estable
Li tirarem lo capèl
Li direm : "Enfant aimable
Venèm vos cantar Noël"
Un farà "Tarara tararèra
Lintampon ladèri tampon
E l'autre farà lo respon :
"Tarara tararèra
Lintampon ladèri tampon"
Novèl vengut pichon popon

Sonatz pifres e trompetas
Timbalas e caramèls,
O vos claras campanetas
Ambe lo còr dels angèls
Digatz-li "Tara tararèra
Lintampon ladèri tampon"
E cadun farà lo respon :
"Tarara tararèra
Lintampon ladèri tampon"
Novèl vengut pichon popon

Jingling Christmas

(English Translation)

We've heard the morning tunes
That have just been played
On golden trumpets
They say it'll be a Daufin (King's son)
One goes : " Tarara tararèra
Lintampon ladèri tampon"
The other answers back:
'Tarara tararèra
Lintampon ladèri tampon"
Welcome, little baby.

When we enter the cowshed
We'll take our hat off for him
We'll say to him "Lovely child,
We've come to sing to you for Christmas"
One will go " Tarara tararèra
Lintampon ladèri tampon"
The other will answer back:
'Tarara tararèra
Lintampon ladèri tampon"
Welcome, little baby.

Play, fifes and trumpets
Timpani and pipes
Or you, clear little bells
Along with the angels choir
Tell him "Tarara tararèra
Lintampon ladèri tampon"
And everyone will answer back:
"Tarara tararèra
Lintampon ladèri tampon"
Welcome, little baby.

Web Resources

You can find more kids songs from Occitania here:

http://www.mamalisa.com/world/occitan.html

18 - Wassail Carol
(Gloucestershire Carol)
English Carol

About Wassail Carol

The WASSAIL carol seems to originate in Gloucestershire, England and it's been around at least since the 17th or 18th century. "Wassail!" is a toast, literally meaning "be in good health". The reply to this is traditionally "Drink-hail!"

Wassailers are carolers who go from door to door carrying a wassail-bowl and singing carols. The wassail-bowl is typically filled with wassail, a spiced ale. The bowl is usually silver and is decorated with ribbons and garlands. The wassailers expect the good people in the house to keep their wassail-bowls full!

Wassail Carol

(English Song)

Wassail! Wassail! all over the town,
Our toast it is white and our ale it is brown;
Our bowl it is made of the white maple tree;
With a wassailing bowl we'll drink to thee.

So here is to Cherry* and to his right cheek
Pray God send our master a good piece of beef
And a good piece of beef that may we all see
With the wassailing bowl, we'll drink to thee.

Here is to Dobbin*, and to his right eye,
God send our master a good Christmas pie;
A good Christmas pie that may we all see,
With a wassailing bowl we'll drink to thee.

So here is to Broad May** and to her broad horn
May God send our master a good crop of corn
And a good crop of corn that may we all see
With the wassailing bowl, we'll drink to thee.

And here is to Fillpail** and to her left ear
Pray God send our master a happy New Year
And a happy New Year as e'er he did see
With the wassailing bowl, we'll drink to thee.

Here is to Colly**, and to her long tail,
Pray God send our master he never may fail
A bowl of strong beer: I pray you draw near,
And our jolly wassail it's then you shall hear.

Come butler, come fill us a bowl of the best
Then we hope that your soul in heaven may rest
But if you do draw us a bowl of the small
Then down shall go butler, bowl and all.

Then here's to the maid in the lily white smock
Who tripped to the door and slipped back the lock
Who tripped to the door and pulled back the pin
For to let these jolly wassailers in.

Wassail wassail!

Notes:

*Cherry and Dobbin are horses

**May, Fillpail and Colly are cows

Web Resources

You can hear a recording of this song here:

http://www.mamalisa.com/blog/?p=140

Web Resources

You can find more kids songs from England here:

http://www.mamalisa.com/world/england.html

19 - Leise rieselt der Schnee (Softly Falls Each Snow Flake) German Song

About Leise rieselt der Schnee

This German Christmas Carol was written by Eduard Ebel (1839-1905) and translated into English by Loralee Jo Kurzius.

Leise rieselt der Schnee (Softly Falls Each Snow Flake)

Leise rieselt der Schnee

(German Song)

Leise rieselt der Schnee,
Still und starr ruht der See,
Weihnachlicht glänzet der wald.
Freue dich,'s Christkind kommt bald!

In den Herzen wird's warm,
Still schweigt Kummer und Harm,
Sorge des lebbens verhalt.
Freue dich,'s Christkind kommt bald!

Bald ist heilige Nacht,
Chor der Engel erwacht,
Hört nur, wie lieblich es schallt:
Freue dich,'s Christkind kommt bald!

Softly Falls Each Snow Flake

(English Translation)

Softly falls each snow flake
Silent and frozen the lake
Christmas shimmers from the moon.
Rejoice the Christ child comes soon!

In our hearts we feel warm
Free from worries and harm
Cares of life fade far away
Come soon dear Christ-Child, we pray!

Soon his journey he'll take
Choir of angels awake
Hear how sublime it does ring
The Christ Child's birth we will sing.

Web Resources

You can listen to a recording and watch a video of this song here:

http://www.mamalisa.com/blog/?p=611

And here:

http://www.mamalisa.com/blog/?p=612

Web Resources

You can find more kids songs from Germany here:

http://www.mamalisa.com/world/germany.html

20 - The Twelve Days of Christmas
December 25 – January 5
English Song

About The Twelve Days of Christmas

Everyone knows the song "The Twelve Days of Christmas". But how many people know what the twelve days actually are?

The Twelve Days of Christmas are actually the 12 days starting with Christmas (December 25th) and ending the day before Epiphany (January 5th). Epiphany is the day the Three Wise Men visited Jesus.

According to Sir James George Frazer in The Golden Bough, his famous 1913 book about mythology, the 12 days of Christmas were considered to correspond to the 12 months of the year. Each (number) day related to the corresponding month. (ie, December 25 was January, December 26 was February, etc.) People even paid attention to the weather of each day and thought that would be the weather of the corresponding month of the upcoming year

Continue on after the familiar version to read about The Twelve Days of Yule, a Scottish variation.

The Twelve Days of Christmas

(English Christmas Carol)

On the first day of Christmas,
my true love sent to me
A partridge in a pear tree.

On the second day of Christmas,
my true love sent to me
Two turtle doves
And a partridge in a pear tree.

On the third day of Christmas,
my true love sent to me
Three French hens,
Two turtledoves
And a partridge in a pear tree.

On the fourth day of Christmas,
my true love sent to me
Four calling birds,
Three French hens,
Two turtle doves
And a partridge in a pear tree.

On the fifth day of Christmas,
my true love sent to me
Five golden rings,
Four calling birds,
Three French hens,
Two turtle doves
And a partridge in a pear tree.

On the sixth day of Christmas,
my true love sent to me
Six geese a-laying,
Five golden rings,
Four calling birds,
Three French hens,
Two turtle doves
And a partridge in a pear tree.

On the seventh day of Christmas,
my true love sent to me
Seven swans a-swimming,

Six geese a-laying,
Five golden rings,
Four calling birds,
Three French hens,
Two turtle doves
And a partridge in a pear tree.

On the eighth day of Christmas,
my true love sent to me
Eight maids a-milking,
Seven swans a-swimming,
Six geese a-laying,
Five golden rings,
Four calling birds,
Three French hens,
Two turtle doves
And a partridge in a pear tree.

On the ninth day of Christmas,
my true love sent to me
Nine ladies dancing,
Eight maids a-milking,
Seven swans a-swimming,
Six geese a-laying,
Five golden rings,
Four calling birds,
Three French hens,
Two turtle doves
And a partridge in a pear tree.

On the tenth day of Christmas,
my true love sent to me
Ten lords a-leaping,
Nine ladies dancing,
Eight maids a-milking,
Seven swans a-swimming,
Six geese a-laying,
Five golden rings,
Four calling birds,
Three French hens,
Two turtle doves
And a partridge in a pear tree.

On the eleventh day of Christmas,
my true love sent to me
Eleven pipers piping,

Ten lords a-leaping,
Nine ladies dancing,
Eight maids a-milking,
Seven swans a-swimming,
Six geese a-laying,
Five golden rings,
Four calling birds,
Three French hens,
Two turtle doves
And a partridge in a pear tree.

On the twelfth day of Christmas,
my true love sent to me
Twelve drummers drumming,
Eleven pipers piping,
Ten lords a-leaping,
Nine ladies dancing,
Eight maids a-milking,
Seven swans a-swimming,
Six geese a-laying,
Five golden rings,
Four calling birds,
Three French hens,
Two turtle doves
And a partridge in a pear tree!

Our correspondent Laura wrote us this wonderful description of the hand geastures that accompany this song...

"1st day...partridge in a pear tree......spread your arms out then bring them up over your head to make the branches of the tree.
2nd day..two turtle doves...hook your thumbs together to form a bird (and then do actions for 1st day)
3rd...three french hens...tuck your hands under your armpits to look like chicken wings and flap (also do previous actions)
4th...Four calling birds...form hands into beaks and open and close your fingers like quacking birds (and previous actions)
5 golden rings...hold up your hand with fingers extended to make it look like you have 5 rings on your fingers (previous actions)
6 geese a laying...make wings out of your arms and shake your butt a little (previous actions)
7 swans a swimming...stand on one foot and raise other foot up to butt and strike a graceful pose (previous actions)
8 maids a milking...acting like you are milking a goat/cow (previous actions)
9 ladies dancing....put your finger on top of your head and dance like a ballerina (and do previous actions)
10 lords a leaping...do ballerina leaps forward(previous actions)
11 pipers piping...act like you are blowing a long horn (previous actions)

12 drummers drumming...act like you are playing a snare drum(and do all previous actions)

I'm not sure if these are the right actions but these are the ones I saw at a grade school concert (so cute)."

Thanks Laura!

Web Resources

You can listen to the tune of this song and print out the sheet music here:

http://www.mamalisa.com/?t=es&p=2499&c=116

The Thirteen Days of Yule (The Twelve Days of Christmas in Scotland)

The 13 Days of Yule was sung in Scotland as far back as the early 1800's, to the tune of The Twelve Days of Christmas.

"Yule" was originally a heathen feast that lasted for 12-13 days. Eventually it came to represent the midwinter season of December and January. Later it became synonymous with Christmas.

Difficult Words

*papingoe = a parrot (though some people think it's a peacock)

**a plover is a type of bird

The Thirteen Days of Yule

The King sent his Lady on the first Yule day,
A papingoe*, aye.
Who learns my carol and carries it away.

The King sent his lady on the second Yule day,
Two partridges and a papingoe, aye.
Who learns my carol and carries it away.

The King sent his lady on the third Yule day,
Three plovers**, three partridges and a papingoe, aye.
Who learns my carol and carries it away.

The King sent his lady on the fourth Yule day,
A goose that was grey,
Three plovers, three partridges and a papingoe, aye.
Who learns my carol and carries it away.

The King sent his lady on the fifth Yule day,
Three starlings, a goose that was grey,
Three plovers, three partridges and a papingoe, aye.
Who learns my carol and carries it away.

The King sent his lady on the sixth Yule day,
Three goldspinks, three starlings, a goose that was grey,
Three plovers, three partridges and a papingoe, aye.
Who learns my carol and carries it away.

The King sent his lady on the seventh Yule day,
A bull that was brown,
Three goldspinks, three starlings, a goose that was grey,
Three plovers, three partridges and a papingoe, aye.
Who learns my carol and carries it away.

The King sent his lady on the eighth Yule day,
Three ducks a-merry laying, a bull that was brown,
Three goldspinks, three starlings, a goose that was grey,
Three plovers, three partridges and a papingoe, aye.
Who learns my carol and carries it away.

The King sent his lady on the ninth Yule day,
Three swans a-merry swimming, three ducks a-merry laying,
A bull that was brown,
Three goldspinks, three starlings, a goose that was grey,
Three plovers, three partridges and a papingoe, aye.
Who learns my carol and carries it away.

The King sent his lady on the tenth Yule day,
An Arabian baboon,
Three swans a-merry swimming, three ducks a-merry laying,
A bull that was brown,
Three goldspinks, three starlings, a goose that was grey,
Three plovers, three partridges and a papingoe, aye.
Who learns my carol and carries it away.

The King sent his lady on the eleventh Yule day,
Three hinds a-merry hunting, an Arabian baboon,
Three swans a-merry swimming, three ducks a-merry laying,
A bull that was brown,
Three goldspinks, three starlings, a goose that was grey,
Three plovers, three partridges and a papingoe, aye.
Who learns my carol and carries it away.

The King sent his lady on the twelfth Yule day,
Three maids a-merry dancing, three hinds a-merry hunting,
An Arabian baboon,
Three swans a-merry swimming, three ducks a-merry laying,
A bull that was brown,
Three goldspinks, three starlings, a goose that was grey,
Three plovers, three partridges and a papingoe, aye.
Who learns my carol and carries it away.

The King sent his lady on the thirteenth Yule day,
Three stalks o merry corn, three maids a-merry dancing,
Three hinds a-merry hunting, an Arabian baboon,
Three swans a-merry swimming, three ducks a-merry laying,
A bull that was brown,
Three goldspinks, three starlings, a goose that was grey,

Three plovers, three partridges and a papingoe, aye.
Who learns my carol and carries it away.

Web Resources

You can find more kids songs from Scotland here:

http://www.mamalisa.com/world/scotland.html

21 - Traditions: Provence
Les Treize Desserts de Noël
(The Thirteen Desserts of Christmas)

Christmas in Provence

At Christmastime in Provence, in the south of France, there's a tradition of having a Christmas meal consisting largely of vegetables, followed by 13 desserts. 13 signifies the number of people at the last supper – Christ and his 12 apostles. The table should be decorated with 3 candlesticks, representing the Trinity. The meal and dessert are eaten before the family goes to midnight mass on Christmas.

Traditionally, a place was also left at the table for one's ancestors. The leftover food was left out all night. This way the ancestors could take part in the meal too. (There's a similar Day of the Dead custom in Mexico, of leaving out food and a place at the table for ancestors.)

It is very important that there are at least 13 desserts – also called LES TREIZE DESSERTS DE NOËL. The 13 desserts can vary depending upon tradition. Generally, they are:

1. Black Nougats – Symbolizing evil – Hard candy made with honey and almonds.

2. White Nougats – Symbolizing good – Soft candy made with sugar, eggs, pistachios, honey, and almonds.

These next four are supposed to symbolize beggars, represented by four religious orders (Franciscans, Dominicans, Carmelite Nuns, Augustinians):

3. Dried Figs

4. Almonds

5. Hazelnuts or other nuts

6. Dried Grapes

The symbol of Mary and Jesus' safe journey from the East:

7. Dates

Some of the other desserts eaten, depending on the region, are:

Oranges

Clementines

Apples

Pears

Grapes

Quince Paste

Melon

Calissons d'Aix (almond-paste pastry with sugar icing)

Oil Cake called Fougasse or Pompe à l'huile (made with Orange Flower Water and Olive Oil)

Finally with these desserts, one drinks cooked wine, representing Jesus himself.

One must have a taste of each dessert to have good luck for the whole year.

Bon appétit!

Thanks to Monique Palomares of Mama Lisa's World en français (www.mamalisa.com/fr) for telling us about this traditon!

Our correspondent Sandra writes...

"Thank you for a wonderful explanation of the French Christmas meal tradition. I was fortunate to have partaken in the christmas meal in 2000. I will never forget all the lovingly prepared food I ate. Now that I know the meaning behind each of the dessert. It makes all these fond memories of France all the more meaningful!"

Monique writes...

"I'd like to add that this is not 'The' French Christmas meal, that it's 'A' French Christmas meal, the one from Provence only. Even if France is a country a little smaller than Texas and we're all French, we all speak French, we all learn the same things at school from North to South and from East to West, we come from different backgrounds: historically and culturally, Provence is not Brittany and Alsace is not Pays Basque, etc. etc. So our traditional dishes are different all over the country, well, like in every country I suppose."

22 - O Tannenbaum
(O Christmas Tree)
German, French and English Song

About O Tannenbaum

O Tannenbaum

O Tannenbaum, the beloved Christmas song, originated in Germany. Versions were sung there as early as the 1500's, but the current form developed in the 1800's. From Germany, the song spread around Europe and to the United States.

Here are several different versions:

First, O Tannenbaum in German.

Since the actual German words are a little different than the way the song O Christmas Tree is sung in English, we've provided a literal English translation of O Tannenbaum. It's interesting to consider that the last line, the German phrase "Dein Kleid will mich was lehren", which literally means "Your dress wants to teach me", doesn't really make sense in English!

That's followed by O Tannenbaum in French, called Mon beau sapin.

And, finally, the best known English version of O Tannenbaum, called O Christmas Tree.

Many thanks to Monique Palomares of Mama Lisa's World en français (www.mamalisa.com/fr) for the German and French versions of O Tannenbaum and for the literal English translation.

We hope you see some beautiful Christmas trees this holiday season!

O Tannenbaum (O Fir Tree)

O Tannenbaum

(German Christmas Carol)

O Tannenbaum, O Tannenbaum,
Wie treu sind deine Blätter
Du grünst nicht nur zur Sommerzeit,
Nein auch im Winter wenn es schneit.
O Tannenbaum, O Tannenbaum,
Wie grün sind deine Blätter!

O Tannenbaum, O Tannenbaum,
Du kannst mir sehr gefallen!
Wie oft hat schon zur Winterszeit
Ein Baum von dir mich hoch erfreut!
O Tannenbaum, O Tannenbaum,
Du kannst mir sehr gefallen!

O Tannenbaum, O Tannenbaum,
Dein Kleid will mich was lehren:
Die Hoffnung und Beständigkeit
Gibt Mut (Trost) und Kraft zu jeder Zeit!
O Tannenbaum, O Tannenbaum,
Dein Kleid will mich was lehren

O Fir Tree

(Literal English Translation of O Tannenbaum)

O fir tree, o fir tree
How true are your leaves
You don't only turn green in summertime
But also in winter, when it snows
O fir tree, o fir tree
How true are your leaves

O fir tree, o fir tree
Much pleasure can you bring me
How often, in winter, a tree of your kind
Has already rejoiced me
O fir tree, o fir tree
Much pleasure can you bring me

O fir tree, o fir tree
Your dress wants to teach me
The hope and the stability
Give courage (comfort) and energy for all time
O fir tree, o fir tree
Your dress wants to teach me.

Web Resources

You can find more kids songs from Germany here:

www.mamalisa.com/world/germany.html

Mon beau sapin

(French Version of O Tannenbaum)

Mon beau sapin, roi des forêts
Que j'aime ta verdure!
Quand, par l'hiver, bois et guérets
Sont dépouillés de leurs attraits
Mon beau sapin, roi des forêts
Tu gardes ta parure.

Toi que Noël planta chez nous
Au saint anniversaire!
Comme ils sont beaux, comme ils sont doux
Et tes bonbons et tes joujoux!
Toi que Noël planta chez nous
Tout brillant de lumière.

Mon beau sapin tes verts sommets
Et leur fidèle ombrage
De la foi qui ne ment jamais
De la constance et de la paix,
Mon beau sapin tes verts sommets
M'offrent la douce image.

Web Resource

You can find more songs from France here:

http://www.mamalisa.com/world/france.html

O Christmas Tree

O Christmas Tree

(English Christmas Carol)

This is the best known English version of O Tannenbaum. It's not as literal a translation as the English version we presented earlier. But it's very beautiful!

O Christmas tree, O Christmas tree!
How are thy leaves so verdant!
O Christmas tree, O Christmas tree,
How are thy leaves so verdant!
Not only in the summertime,
But even in winter is thy prime.
O Christmas tree, O Christmas tree,
How are thy leaves so verdant!

O Christmas tree, O Christmas tree,
Much pleasure doth thou bring me!
O Christmas tree, O Christmas tree,
Much pleasure doth thou bring me!
For every year the Christmas tree,
Brings to us all both joy and glee.
O Christmas tree, O Christmas tree,
Much pleasure doth thou bring me!

O Christmas tree, O Christmas tree,
Thy candles shine out brightly!
O Christmas tree, O Christmas tree,
Thy candles shine out brightly!
Each bough doth hold its tiny light,
That makes each toy to sparkle bright.
O Christmas tree, O Christmas tree,
Thy candles shine out brightly!

23 - Jest 'fore Christmas
English Poem

About Jest 'fore Christmas

Eugene Field (1850-1895), has been one of America's best-loved children's poets for over 100 years,. His most famous works include "Little Boy Blue", "Wynken, Blynken, and Nod" and "The Duel".

At Christmas time, fans of Eugene Field particularly enjoy "Jest 'fore Christmas". Here it is...

Jest 'fore Christmas

(English Poem)

Father calls me William, sister calls me Will,
Mother calls me Willie, but the fellers call me Bill!
Mighty glad I ain't a girl—ruther be a boy,
Without them sashes, curls, an' things that's worn by Fauntleroy!
Love to chawnk green apples an' go swimmin' in the lake—
Hate to take the castor-ile they give for bellyache!
'Most all the time, the whole year round, there ain't no flies on me,
But jest 'fore Christmas I'm as good as I kin be!

Got a yeller dog named Sport, sick him on the cat;
First thing she knows she doesn't know where she is at!
Got a clipper sled, an' when us kids goes out to slide,
'Long comes the grocery cart, an' we all hook a ride!
But sometimes when the grocery man is worrited an' cross,
He reaches at us with his whip, an' larrups up his hoss,
An' then I laff an' holler, "Oh, ye never teched me!"
But jest 'fore Christmas I'm as good as I kin be!

Gran'ma says she hopes that when I git to be a man,
I'll be a missionarer like her oldest brother, Dan,
As was et up by the cannibuls that lives in Ceylon's Isle,
Where every prospeck pleases, an' only man is vile!
But gran'ma she has never been to see a Wild West show,
Nor read the Life of Daniel Boone, or else I guess she'd know
That Buff'lo Bill an' cowboys is good enough for me!
Excep' jest 'fore Christmas, when I'm good as I kin be!

And then old Sport he hangs around, so solemnlike an' still,
His eyes they seem a-sayin': "What's the matter, little Bill?"
The old cat sneaks down off her perch an' wonders what's become
Of them two enemies of hern that used to make things hum!
But I am so perlite an' tend so earnestly to biz,
That mother says to father: "How improved our Willie is!"
But father, havin' been a boy hisself, suspicions me
When, jest 'fore Christmas, I'm as good as I kin be!

For Christmas, with its lots an' lots of candies, cakes, an' toys,
Was made, they say, for proper kids an' not for naughty boys;
So wash yer face an' bresh yer hair, an' mind yer p's and q's,
An' don't bust out yer pantaloons, and don't wear out yer shoes;
Say "Yessum" to the ladies, and "Yessur" to the men,
An' when they's company, don't pass yer plate for pie again;
But, thinkin' of the things yer'd like to see upon that tree,
Jest 'fore Christmas be as good as yer kin be!

So remember to be good boys and girls! Santa Claus is coming to town!

Happy Holidays From All Of Us At Mama Lisa's World!

Made in the USA
Las Vegas, NV
10 December 2022